Humpback Whale Migration

by Kari Schuetz

BLASTOFF! READERS
3

BELLWETHER MEDIA • MINNEAPOLIS, MN

Note to Librarians, Teachers, and Parents:

Blastoff! Readers are carefully developed by literacy experts and combine standards-based content with developmentally appropriate text.

Level 1 provides the most support through repetition of high-frequency words, light text, predictable sentence patterns, and strong visual support.

Level 2 offers early readers a bit more challenge through varied simple sentences, increased text load, and less repetition of high-frequency words.

Level 3 advances early-fluent readers toward fluency through increased text and concept load, less reliance on visuals, longer sentences, and more literary language.

Level 4 builds reading stamina by providing more text per page, increased use of punctuation, greater variation in sentence patterns, and increasingly challenging vocabulary.

Level 5 encourages children to move from "learning to read" to "reading to learn" by providing even more text, varied writing styles, and less familiar topics.

Whichever book is right for your reader, Blastoff! Readers are the perfect books to build confidence and encourage a love of reading that will last a lifetime!

This edition first published in 2019 by Bellwether Media, Inc.

No part of this publication may be reproduced in whole or in part without written permission of the publisher. For information regarding permission, write to Bellwether Media, Inc., Attention: Permissions Department, 6012 Blue Circle Drive, Minnetonka, MN 55343.

Library of Congress Cataloging-in-Publication Data

Names: Schuetz, Kari, author.
Title: Humpback Whale Migration / by Kari Schuetz.
Description: Minneapolis, MN : Bellwether Media, Inc., 2019. | Series: Blastoff! Readers. Animals on the Move | Audience: Age 5-8. | Audience: Grade K to 3. | Includes bibliographical references and index.
Identifiers: LCCN 2017061806 (print) | LCCN 2018005323 (ebook) | ISBN 9781626178168 (hardcover : alk. paper) | ISBN 9781681035574 (ebook)
Subjects: LCSH: Humpback whale--Migration--Juvenile literature.
Classification: LCC QL737.C424 (ebook) | LCC QL737.C424 S38 2019 (print) | DDC 599.5/251568--dc23
LC record available at https://lccn.loc.gov/2017061806

Editor: Paige V. Polinsky   Designer: Jeffrey Kollock

Printed in the United States of America, North Mankato, MN

Table of Contents

Humpback Whales

Humpback whales are mighty distance swimmers. Year after year, these ocean giants move back and forth between faraway waters.

Humpback Whale Profile

animal type: mammal

habitat: oceans

size: body length: 40 to 60 feet
(12 to 18 meters)
weight: up to 80,000 pounds
(36,287 kilograms)

life span: 50 to 80 years

They **migrate** farther than just about every other traveling **mammal**!

These whales have a **torpedo** shape. This helps them slide smoothly through water.

tail fin

side fin →

Their strong tail fins move up and down to push them forward. Long side fins control direction and speed.

Warmer Waters

Humpback whales feed in **polar** waters. But **calves** must be born and raised in warmer waters.

Mealtime ends in the fall. The whales must travel to their winter birthing grounds.

calf

Humpback Whale Departure

mode of travel: swimming

arriving winter: tropical waters

leaving fall: polar waters

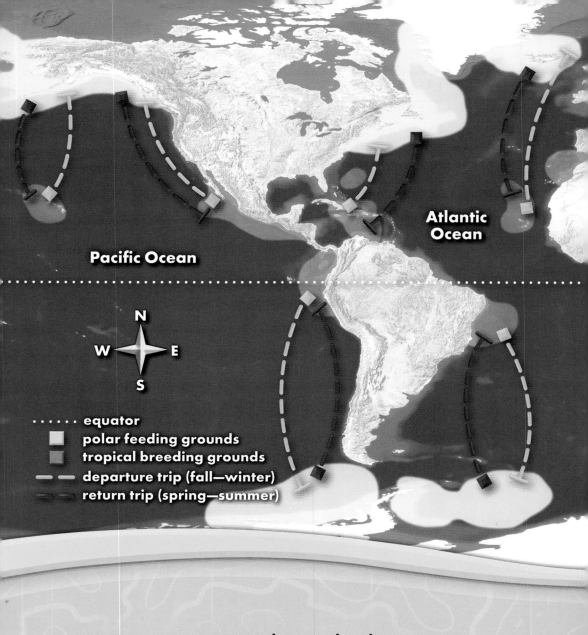

Pacific Ocean

N
W   E
S

····· equator
⬜ polar feeding grounds
🟫 tropical breeding grounds
— — departure trip (fall—winter)
▪ ▪ return trip (spring—summer)

To migrate, the whales
swim toward the **equator**.
Some swim alone.

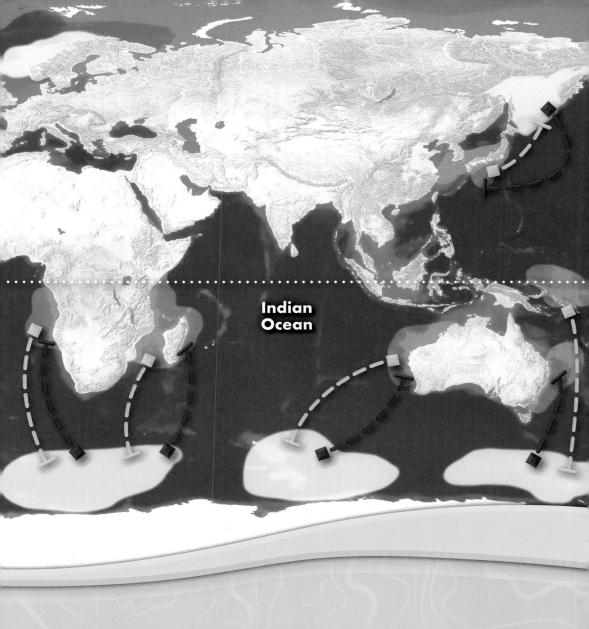

Indian
Ocean

Other whales form brief travel
pods of two or three. Growing
calves always stick with their moms.

Just Below the Surface

Humpback whales can hold their breath for 45 minutes. Then they need air.

The whales stay near the water's surface during their trips. This makes it easy to breathe through their **blowholes**.

blowholes

Sometimes boats hit humpbacks by mistake. Fishing nets can trap them, too.

spy-hopping

breaching

The whales **spy-hop** to spot danger above the surface. A **breach** might be a warning to others.

After about one month, the whales reach **tropical** waters. There, they often form pods of up to twenty whales.

Humpback Whale Dashboard

speed: up to 16 mph (26 km/h)

mph = miles per hour km/h = kilometers per hour

miles traveled per year:

1	1	7	0	6

(18,839 kilometers)

miles traveled per day:

-	-	-	8	5

(137 kilometers)

Males sing and compete for females. **Pregnant** females give birth to calves.

Feeding Time

Humpback whales do not eat all winter. By spring, they are hungry! They swim back to polar waters for food.

The whales open their mouths wide to eat. Stiff hairs inside trap **krill** and small fish.

krill

Humpback Whale Return

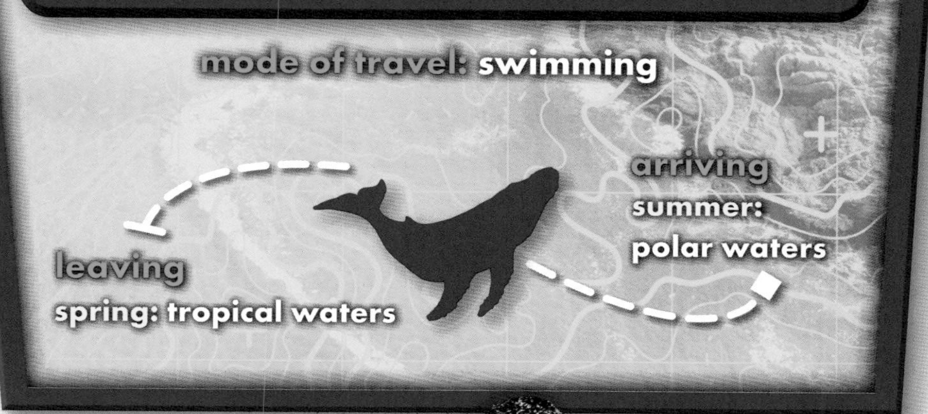

mode of travel: swimming

leaving
spring: tropical waters

arriving
summer:
polar waters

19

Sometimes humpbacks work together to catch a feast. First, they circle a group of fish. Then they blow bubbles.

This bubble net traps their meal. The whales must fill up before they migrate again!

bubble net

Glossary

blowholes—the holes on top of a humpback whale's head that are used for breathing

breach—a leap out of the water

calves—baby humpback whales

equator—the imaginary line around the center of Earth

krill—small, shrimplike ocean animals

mammal—a warm-blooded animal that has a backbone and feeds its young milk

migrate—to travel from one place to another, often with the seasons

pods—groups of humpback whales

polar—related to the northernmost or southernmost area of Earth

pregnant—expecting a baby

spy-hop—to rise straight up and poke just the head above the water's surface

torpedo—a tube-shaped weapon fired underwater

tropical—related to the tropics; the tropics is a hot region near the equator.

To Learn More

AT THE LIBRARY

Leaf, Christina. *Humpback Whales*. Minneapolis, Minn.: Bellwether Media, 2017.

Polinsky, Paige V. *Humpback Whale: Marvelous Musician*. Minneapolis, Minn.: ABDO Publishing, 2017.

Tunby, Benjamin. *The Whale's Journey*. Minneapolis, Minn.: Lerner Publications, 2018.

ON THE WEB

Learning more about humpback whale migration is as easy as 1, 2, 3.

1. Go to www.factsurfer.com.

2. Enter "humpback whale migration" into the search box.

3. Click the "Surf" button and you will see a list of related web sites.

With factsurfer.com, finding more information is just a click away.

Index

The images in this book are reproduced through the courtesy of: Tomas Kotouc, front cover (whale), p. 4; Dimitri Vaindirlis, front cover (gradient map); Michael Smith ITWP, pp. 4-5; Dave Fleethamd/Pacific Stock/ SuperStock, p. 5; wildestanimal, p. 6; Paul S. Wolf, p. 7; Yann hubert, p. 8; MZPHOTO.CZ, p. 9; le bouil baptiste, p. 12; Jay Ondreicka, p. 13; Bluegreen Pictures/ Alamy, p. 14; jiawangkun, p. 15; Kerstin Meyer/ Getty, p. 16; Dmytro Pylypenko, p. 18; Adam Stockland, p. 19; Carl Thompson/ EyeEm/ Getty, p. 20; Arterra Picture Library/ Alamy, p. 21.